When God Got His Hands Dirty

and other thoughts about the God Who wants to hang out with us

By Jill Libramento

Text copyright ©2016 Jill Libramento

All Rights Reserved

All scripture references are from New International Version unless otherwise indicated.

Table of Contents

When God Got His Hands Dirty

When God Got Blood on His Hands

The Day After

Dreaming With God

When God Went Camping

When God Put on a Play

When God Wasn't Embarrassed

When Jesus Spit and Got His Hands Dirty Again

When Jesus Cooked Breakfast

When God Lives With Us

When God Met Me On The Beach

Preface

There are so many things I love about God but one thing that simultaneously breaks and heals my heart is God reaching down to man. God Almighty, Maker of heaven and earth, the One Who Was and Is and Is to Come, the Ancient of Days, the Sustainer of life, Love Incarnate stepping away from all the glory that is His and moving close to us. He's done it so many times and He does it every day. The One Who is the purest and holiest embraces the vilest creature.

There's a meme on of Steve Irwin holding some sort of scaly creature. I can never remember the difference between a crocodile and an alligator. It might even be a caiman, one of those things. Anyway, he's holding it lovingly next to his face with an expression of pure delight and love and the words say: "Knows everything in Australia wants to kill him. Picks them up, hugs them and tells them how beautiful they are." It makes me laugh and cry and makes my heart say, "Yes! That's the way God is!" Steve's unbridled passion and love for animals was a beautiful and terrifying thing to behold.

God's unbridled love and passion is also a beautiful and terrifying thing to behold. It also makes my heart leap, brings tears to my eyes and makes me laugh at His Holy Audacity. When I point out the times that God takes off His Glory to move closer to us, I speak of it with the utmost respect and gratitude. I realize He doesn't have to do it. It is at a great cost. And it is out of unfathomable love. I am not trying to bring Him down to our level, I kneel in humility that He comes to our level willingly.

There's no mocking in my heart when it comes to this topic, only admiration, awe and gratitude.

Peace,

Jill

When God Got His Hands Dirty

"Then the Lord God formed man of dust from the ground, and breathed into his nostrils the breath of life; and man became a living being. The Lord God planted a garden toward the east in Eden; and there He placed the man whom He had formed." Genesis 2:7-8 NAS

Have you ever noticed that everything that was created was spoken into existence except for man and the garden? His omnipotent, creative, life-giving Word created it all: sun, moon, stars, galaxies, land, seas, beasts, birds, plants. He spoke and the atoms, molecules, elements and energy all fell in line. That was how He did it. Except when it came to man, why?

I think I know why. My father-in-law is a craftsman. He works with wood. He makes chairs and spoons and bowls among other things. I like to watch his hands when he works. He touches the wood like he's communicating with it. He feels the grain. He feels the hardness or softness of the wood. As he's working with it, he's constantly feeling it to determine if it's becoming what he envisions. Touching it is necessary and significant. That's why a handcrafted item is more valuable than a machine-made item. It's more personal. The maker envisions it, handles it, and is right there through the process of creation to final product.

After I gave birth to my children I wanted to touch them. I smelled them. I listened to them. I had to feel them in my arms. I had to have my hands on them as much as possible. It gave me joy. I traced my daughter's face with my finger. I caressed my son's beautiful hands and soft ears. Even as adults I just can't help touching them, hugging them, walking arm and arm with them where ever we go.

God is a craftsman and a father. The word "formed" in Hebrew describes a potter molding a vessel. God could have spoken man into existence like He did everything else. But man, this creation, needed special attention. God, like a craftsman, had a vision and nothing would do but that He gathered the dust in His own hands and did it Himself. Like a CEO rolling up his sleeves and getting his hands into the work he usually delegates, God became intimately involved in the creation of man. Dust is on the ground. Dust is dirty. God knelt down and got His hands dirty to make man. And then He breathed His own life into the man. The breath of God, imagine that.

After God made man I'm sure He couldn't keep His hands off of him. God is a Father after all. God probably brushed man's hair out of his eyes and wiped dirt off his cheek. I'm sure there was hugging and laughing and slapping each other on the back. Then after He made the man, like a true Father, God modeled for man what He wanted him to do. God planted a garden. Again, God got His hands dirty. He dug holes and took the plants and seeds and puts them in the ground. He taught man how to do it because that's what man was going to do: tend the garden. Isn't that wonderful? The first job that God gave man to do was tend a garden. Tend the garden that God planted. His job wasn't to start businesses, build cities, conquer lands or wage wars. (I know there were no other people at the time, just roll with me.) He simply had to take care of what God had made. And it was in this garden where God and man would walk and talk in the cool of the evening. That lovely place they shared. God and man, Father and child, Creator and creation.

Then man broke God's heart. They were separated. No more walks. No more talks. No more hugs and slaps on the back. No more digging in the dirt together. Adam wept. God wept.

When God Got Blood on His Hands

"They heard the sound of the Lord God walking in the garden in the cool of the day, and the man and his wife hid themselves from the presence of the Lord among the trees of the garden." Genesis3:8 NAS

I can't continue talking about God moving near to us, overcoming obstacles to get to us, or His desire to be with us, without stopping at this day of separation. God and man, Father and child, best friends– separated. The heartbreak of that day can't be ignored.

I'm not a theologian but I am a student of human nature and I know a little about the heart of God. I know God had a plan, an overall plan to redeem mankind, however, I also know God and Adam had hearts. And I believe their hearts were broken that day. Even though it was in the plan, it was still a day they lived, a day they felt.

One evening, in that wonderful, magical time after the sun has gone down but it's not totally dark, when the fireflies come out and the best time to play hide-and-seek, God came down to spend time with Adam. Adam was hiding but it was not a game.

Adam messed up and he knew it. Adam was afraid. How will God react? He blamed the woman. The woman blamed the serpent. God got angry. Really angry! Not a personal offense kind of angry, but a "this can't be undone" angry. He turned on the serpent first, then the woman and finally Adam. I imagine that towards the end of this terminal diagnosis tears flowed from His eyes. The reality and finality of it hit Him. His child, His friend will now be doomed to die. His words will come true and real just as they did at creation.

"You will eat bread, till you return to the ground, because from it you were taken; for you are dust and to dust you shall return."

I can see God walk away leaving Adam and Eve in shock. They probably wondered where He was going. I imagine Adam, still longing to be near, still wishing his could say something to make it right again, but afraid of God's anger, followed at a distance. He watched God walk into the meadow among the grazing sheep. God gently picked up a lamb, a beautiful, perfect lamb. He pulled it close to his chest and nuzzled His face in its wool. He knelt on the ground, the lamb sniffed God's chin. God lifted the lamb's head and Adam saw a knife in God's hand. Bright red blood flooded the lambs neck and chest and it slumped as if it has fallen asleep. Adam sunk to his knees in shock. "What did God just do?" Nothing had ever died, much less been killed since it was created. They had never even cut down a tree or uprooted a plant except to move it to a better place where it could thrive.

Maybe hours passed and Adam watched God through the shrub as He skinned the lamb and fashioned something out of it. He took the dead lamb, made a fire and burned its body on it. God watched the sacrifice burn to ashes. Adam wondered what He was thinking about or remembering.

Finally, God turned and Adam and Eve rushed to meet Him at the edge of the garden. God called them from their hiding among the trees and He gave them the clothes He had made for them. His hands still tinted from the blood. Adam cried. He was overwhelmed by the embarrassment of being naked and the guilt of what he had done. Feeling the soft wool against his skin, he could hardly breathe at the thought that an innocent lamb had to die to cover his shame.

When they had dressed, God told them to leave. He wasn't loud or angry. He just told them they had to go. They had to fend for themselves. They had work the ground and make their own way. Eve broke down. Adam cried, "No! Please don't make us go! I don't want to leave You!" Adam hung on to God's feet. At this, God was moved, with tears in His eyes He shouted, "You have to go!" The tone of His voice, a mixture of disappointment and determination, let Adam know he had no other choice. He gathered Eve in his arms and they left. Eve turned to run back into the garden but with a wave of God's hand an angel appeared with a flaming sword. No matter which way Eve tried to get past him, the angel moved in front of her. Beyond the angel and Eve's desperate dance, Adam could see God. God bowed His head and walked away among the trees. Adam thought he knew where He would go. They had met there every evening. The pain in Adam's chest made him feel like he had never felt before. He could barely breathe. Is this what death feels like? He wondered. Eve finally gave up in a heap on the ground and again Adam gathered her up and they went on their way.

The Day After

"So He drove the man out; and at the east of the garden of Eden He stationed the cherubim and the flaming sword which turned every direction to guard the way to the tree of life." Genesis 3:24 NAS

The day that God and man separated was difficult indeed. However, the day after was horrid in its own way. Can you imagine if all you had ever known was being surrounded by lush, green, sweet vegetation with ripe fruits and vegetables at hand, anytime you wanted them and then waking up one morning faced with a barren, dry wasteland before you? Every hunger pang, every sore muscle, every drop of sweat reminding you of what you had lost? And that's not the worst of it - every evening - silence. The silence Adam lived in was so loud he couldn't hear anything else. The void that God's absence left was so big that it smothered him.

God didn't come to walk and talk anymore. Adam was alone. Yes, he had Eve and the children they had together but this was a different kind of lonely. This was that soul-lonely that no human can fix.

Adam kept busy doing what he knew to do, planting gardens. He was able to feed his family. It was difficult at first but it got better as time went on. He learned times and seasons and developed techniques for watering and fertilizing. It was heartbreaking to see the plants and animals fight to survive and then die knowing that it didn't used to be that way. They were dying because of him. He kept his mind off of it by being busy during the day, but the evenings were the worst.

Adam had never seen where God went during the day. When He had asked God where He lived, God would look up to the sky. So, every evening around the time that God used to come down to walk and talk, Adam would sit under the stars.

Sometimes he would lay back and stare so long that he thought he saw God out of the corner of his eye. Sometimes he would doze off and in that space between being awake and being asleep Adam thought he felt God lying beside him. Sometimes he thought he heard his voice in the sound of the nearby waterfall or smell His breath on the breeze.

The historian, Josephus, said that Seth, Adam's son and his children were "inventors of that peculiar sort of wisdom which is concerned with the heavenly bodies, and their order." I wonder if Seth learned that from his father as they lay together night after night looking in the sky hoping to see God.

Dreaming With God

"And He took him outside and said, "Now look toward the heavens, and count the stars, if you are able to count them" And He said to him, "So shall your descendants be."Genesis 15:5 NAS

On the other side of the expanse of heaven I imagine God looking down at Adam longing to come down and walk and talk with him again. But things had changed.

God watched over Adam, silently. He sent the rains, He sent the harvest, He sent signs in the heavens. He watched proudly as Adam figured out His codes and discovered His secrets.

When Adam had returned to the dust, God watched over Adam's children. He watched them use the rains, harvest and signs for their own gain. They stopped making sacrifices and stopped looking for Him in the heavens.

Then one evening, as God was making His journey across the heavens pulling the indigo blanket of night across the sky, He noticed a man staring at the sky, looking for Him. His name was Abram.

God kept His eye on Abram. Abram kept looking for God. He knew in his gut that God was out there, somewhere. Even when his family and friends made fun of him, Abram kept looking. Even when his wife would yell at him to come inside and quit staring at the sky like a fool, Abram kept looking. Abram made God smile. God liked him.

When Abram's father died, he was sad and lost and afraid because he was now the head of the family. He'd never be able to live up to his father's leadership. He didn't know what to do or where to go. In his fear and frustration, he went outside, looked at the sky and cried out, "Where are You? I need You! I know You're there!" God's heart was moved and like a good Father he went to his child's side and gave him direction and hope and strength. God told Abram things and Abram believed Him. God would direct Him and Abram would do it. They became good friends.

One night, alone in his tent, Abram was grieving. His shame and sadness over not having a child was drowning him. God's heart was moved. God came to him, took him outside and they lay on the hillside staring at the stars together. God said to Abram, "Now look toward the heavens, and count the stars, if you are able to count them. So shall your descendants be." Abram was speechless. I imagine God turned toward Abram and smiled because Abram really believed Him.

There they were, God and Abram, lying on the hillside dreaming together - dreaming of their children. I imagine that Abram began imagining all the kids running around his feet. He chuckled as he thought of Sarai yelling and shooing them out of the tent. He thought of all the piggy back rides and tickle fights. I believe his chest was filled with pride as he imagined them all. In each twinkling star, Abram saw the face of each one of his children. With each flicker of light he heard their laugh and gave them each a name.

In my imagination I see God lying there, too, and in each twinkling star he saw our face, heard our laugh and whispered our name.

When God Went Camping

"Let them construct a sanctuary for Me, that I may dwell among them." Exodus 25:8

I think most people have this view of God as high and lifted up, living in the heavens, holy and untouchable on His throne. Some may feel He is out of touch with our real lives down here because He's not here, He's up there. Some may picture Him as bored or tired and only getting involved when He absolutely has to like we are an annoyance, a bother to Him. Still others might think of Him as arrogant and haughty, too good to mingle among us filthy lowlanders.

However, God's desire to hang out with us, to live with us, to love us is so great that none of what I just said is true. We can see it when He told Moses that He wanted the Israelites to make a Tabernacle for Him so He could live among them as they traveled in the wilderness. Have you ever been camping? It's not pretty. It's dirty and smelly and the bathroom situation and bathing is a real challenge. The cooking situation is not very sanitary and there's smoke and ashes. It's always too hot and too cold and there's the dew making everything all wet in the morning. People are uncomfortable and on edge and there's usually griping and complaining. And let's not forget the wildlife and dangerous plant component. Camping is seriously roughing it. But God decided to leave all His glory in heaven and go camping with His people.

The story of the Tabernacle begins in such an amazing way. In Exodus 24 we read this: *"Moses and Aaron, Nadab and Abihu and seventy elders of Israel went up and saw the God of Israel.* (they SAW Him!) *Under His feet was something like a pavement made of sapphire, clear as the sky itself. But God did not raise His hand against these leaders of the Israelites; they saw God and they ate and drank."* What? These guys got to have dinner with God? Incredible! Then after dinner, God pulled Moses aside and told him to come further up the mountain. Moses and God hung out for forty days and forty nights. Now, this wasn't just hanging out, this was work. God laid out plans for His tent, how it should be designed, the materials to use and all that. I picture Moses furiously taking notes and making sketches. He was trained in that, you know, being raised as the son of Pharaoh, being around all that construction in Egypt and organizing projects. Just think, being able to work on a project with God!

The Israelites had just left Egypt. They're on the road and on the run. Now they're going to build a tent for God with very specific requirements. There were a lot of gold and precious jewels required and some very strange and specific things needed like ram skins dyed red and the hides of sea cows. Where did they get this stuff? God planned ahead. Remember when they were leaving Egypt and after all the scary plagues? Remember the Egyptians were freaked out about the Hebrews and their God? God told Moses to tell the people as they were leaving to ask the Egyptians for silver, gold and articles of clothing. The Egyptians eagerly gave the Israelites what they had and *"so they plundered the Egyptians. (Exodus 12:36 NIV)"* Back wages, I guess.

So, out there in the desert they had all the materials they needed to make God a tent so He could live with them. God set up sacrifices and rules and requirements so that the people would be safe with God living among them. God's holiness destroys sin, so they had to make sure they stayed pure so God could keep living with them and they wouldn't die. And He did. God came down and dwelled in the tent they had made. *"So the cloud of the Lord was over the tabernacle by day and fire was in the cloud by night, in the sight of all the house of Israel during all their travels. (Exodus 40:38 NIV)"*

God's presence kept them cool in the day and warm at night. How kind of Him to do that.

God traveled with the Israelites. He stayed with them through thick and thin. He stayed with them when they rebelled, when they complained, when they messed up. He stayed and loved them. Oh, He got angry, but He stayed. When things got difficult He didn't pack up His tent and go home. He stuck it out. That's what family does. That's what friends do.

When I think of being a friend of God I can't help but think of Moses. *"The Lord would speak to Moses face to face, as a man speaks with his friend. (Exodus 33:11 NIV)"* What a man Moses must have been! Educated and trained in the wealthiest, most culturally rich and most powerful nation of the world at the time. To top it off he was raised in the household of Pharaoh having access the best of everything! Can you imagine the military, architectural and political skills and experience he had? What about his courage to leave all that and align himself with slaves against Pharaoh and all Egypt. I think Moses was creative, too. He wrote songs and sang them. I'm sure he discussed design, color and form with Bezalel and Oholiab, the guys God appointed to design and decorate the Tabernacle and all the furniture in it. Not only that, but Moses was able to execute all of God's requests, fulfill all God's requirements and meet with God face to face as a friend. I imagine that Moses was a man of strong character, dedication and passion. Moses was the man!

I think God thought so, too, because at the end of Moses' life, God took him to Mount Pisgah and showed him the land that God promised. You know Moses couldn't enter the Promised Land because of his disobedience at the Desert of Zin. But God didn't disown Moses or reject him. They were friends. So, even though he couldn't go in, God still allowed him to see it. They had worked so hard to get there. After seeing it, Moses died on that mount at 120 years old. He was still strong, *"his eyes were not weak nor his strength gone. (Deuteronomy 34:7)"* I think about God and Moses on that mountain alone. What did they talk about? Maybe they talked about all their adventures together. Maybe they laughed. Maybe they cried. Maybe they were sad that it would be different and they would miss each other. I think they talked like the good friends they were and then Moses fell asleep. Then God dug a hole, again getting His hands dirty, picked up His friend and buried him.

When God Put on a Play

"He said to me, 'Son of man, stand up on your feet and I will speak to you."Ezekiel 2:1

I've always been so amazed that God includes people in His plans. I often wonder why the Omnipotent, Omniscient, Omnipresent Almighty would involve such weak, vulnerable and mistake-ridden beings in His work. It astounds me! However, it is explained in 1 Corinthians 1:26-29, *"Brothers and sisters think of what you were when you were called. Not many of you were wise by human standards; not many were influential; not many were of noble birth. But God chose the foolish things of the world to shame the wise; God chose the weak things of the world to shame the strong. God chose the lowly things of this world and the despised things - and the things that are not - to nullify the things that are, so that no one may boast before Him."* Our weakness really does highlight His greatness.

I have noticed that God often calls those who struggle to speak whether from a physical hindrance or emotional one, to speak for Him. I have noticed that a lot of worship leaders fight stage fright and shyness. He calls the fearful to be brave, the anxious to be bold. He calls us to work alongside Him so that we can be healed and stronger and braver and by that He is glorified. We see this often in scripture. So, it makes me wonder about Ezekiel, the man who worked with God to put on a play.

Ezekiel 2:4-6 tells us that God called Ezekiel to help Him and told him right up front that there would be challenges. *"The people to whom I am sending you are obstinate and stubborn. Say to them, 'This is what the Sovereign Lord says.' And whether they listen or fail to listen*

– for they are a rebellious people – they will know that a prophet has been among them. And you, son of man, do not be afraid of them or their words. Do not be afraid, though briers and thorns are all around you and you live among scorpions. Do not be afraid of what they say or be terrified by them, though they are a rebellious people." God repeats to Ezekiel that he should speak even if they listen or fail to listen. He lets Ezekiel know that the message may not go over very well and he may not feel successful.

I get the impression that maybe Ezekiel was a little shy, a people–pleaser, nervous, maybe a bit wishy-washy. Maybe he didn't like confrontation because God tells Ezekiel how he would be transformed through working on this project with Him: *"But I will make you as unyielding and hardened as they are. I will make your forehead like the hardest stone, harder than flint. Do not be afraid of them or terrified by them, though they are a rebellious people (vs. 8-9).*

The project that was going to change Ezekiel was a series of one-man performance art pieces that was going to shock and surprise those hard, rebellious people. Now, these were legitimate performances for they had all the elements of theatre. There was an audience, (God says these things should be done *"in the sight of the people."*), a performer, a script or message and an element of pretend meaning that the event was not actually happening at the moment.

In chapter 4 we read about the first piece God and Ezekiel worked on together. It was a prophetic performance about the Siege of Jerusalem. Now, I won't go into all the details of the performance itself, but rather about how God and Ezekiel worked together. God had an idea of what He wanted the people of Israel to know. He thought it would be best communicated by a mime of a siege followed by a long (over a year long) production of life in exile. That is a long continuous run!

So, God communicated to Ezekiel His idea for the production. We don't get any indication that Ezekiel balks at the length of the performance nor the endurance that would be required of him but he does have a problem with the part where he has to bake his bread over human excrement. Ezekiel lets God know that he doesn't want to defile himself for this project. God replied, *"Very well, I will let you bake your bread over cow dung instead."* This is creative collaboration. I'm humbled at this picture of God and man working creatively together.

If you continue to read through the book of Ezekiel you'll find more accounts of guerrilla theatre. There are accounts of aggressive, in-your-face pieces of performance art written by God, performed by Ezekiel for the Children of Israel. I am sure the audience ridiculed him, made fun of him and rejected him as a mad man. God told him ahead of time it would happen. God had to make him strong, brave and hard to endure the criticism. We are not given any indication if the Children of Israel took the messages to heart and changed their ways. The results are not our responsibility, but God's.

If I had understood God's way of "changing us through the doing" years ago, I might have fought Him less, doubted Him less and had it a bit easier when He asked me to do things. We are taught that you have to go to school, learn a trade, be educated, get trained in a skill before you put yourself out there. However, God works differently. He gives us on the job training. I think the reason it is so challenging to work with God in that way is because in order to do it we have to humble ourselves. We have to admit that we don't know what we're doing and we have to trust Him. I'm laughing as I type this because why do we even act like we know what we're doing anyway? Life is an improv. We're all making this up as we go along. Oh, we can get advice from people but no one in the world has your unique set of circumstances, your personality, your experience. No one can tell you exactly how to raise your child or love your spouse, what job to take, what house to buy. Only God knows you. Only God understands all your baggage. Only God sees the incredible person you can be if you let Him change you in the doing. Remember God is the Author of your play. He is the *"Author and Perfecter of our faith…*(Hebrews 12:2)"

When God Wasn't Embarrassed

> *"Mary was pledged to be married to Joseph, but before they came together, she was found to be pregnant through the Holy Spirit." Matthew 1:18*

I got saved when I was 12 and then had an encounter with God when I was 22. At that time God spoke to me and I began to see the difference between God's demands and man's demands on us as Christians. God stripped me of what man had put on me and ever since then my journey has been one of not allowing Christian convention to control me, but rather the Spirit. Like Paul, there are things that I do and don't do so as not to offend a brother. But my basic modus operandi is very simple: love.

I like God. I like that He's giant and powerful. I like that He created everything. I like that He can do whatever He wants to. I like that He's so good that we don't have to worry about Him doing things that are evil and cruel. I like that God is mysterious. I like that He's surprising. I like that with all that power and glory He still likes to hang out with the common folk. It makes my heart burn with love and tears of joy fill my eyes to know that He's like that. I like that we cannot confine or trap God. He is just free. The story of Jesus becoming man is one of those moments where God blows our minds. God becoming man is mind blowing enough, but how He becomes man is like getting a gift you didn't expect, when you least expected it. You are excited and surprised all at the same time.

Jesus became human by being born from a young, unmarried girl. She was engaged to be married, but not married yet. She got pregnant and it looked to everyone around her that she had been unfaithful, a bad girl. Not only that but her child will be illegitimate, born out of wedlock. God was coming down to earth. The King of Kings was becoming human. The Creator wanted to be with His people but He doesn't make a grand entrance, a huge scene. He comes looking like an illegitimate child, a poor outcast. And you know what? It doesn't bother Him in the least. He's not embarrassed. It was just what He wanted to do. What kind of God is that?

He's the kind of God who's not ashamed of you. All the stuff that people put on you about how you should dress, how you should talk, how you should act to impress, to influence, doesn't matter to God at all. He doesn't care where you come from. He wants to hang out with you. He's not ashamed to be seen with you. He's glad for people to know that you and He are friends. That's the kind of God He is.

God became a man. He got His hands dirty, His feet dirty. He laughed. He cried. He cut His finger, He stubbed His toe. He hugged. He kissed. He ate good food. He drank bad wine. Our pain troubles Him. Our joy gladdens Him. He sees the good, the bad and the ugly and still He longs to gather His people under His wings like a hen gathers her chicks. He wants to hang out with us.

When Jesus Spit and Got His Hands Dirty Again

"One thing I do know. I was blind but now I see." John 9:25

One thing I was concerned about when I sat down to write this book was how educated people might shred it to pieces and challenge my theology. I didn't set out to write this as a theological or doctrinal teaching. I just wanted to share how I perceive God, how He's revealed Himself to me. I thought it might provide a breath of fresh air for some. Not everyone. *"For those who have eyes let them see."* I'm like the man born blind whom Jesus healed. He couldn't answer all the questions the Pharisees put to him, but He could confess that once he was blind but now he can see.

Jesus was born into Jewish culture, the culture that He as God established. He set the Sabbath rules. "Don't work on the Sabbath." Then people began to decide what He meant by "work." I guess they decided that spitting in the dirt and making mud was "work" so when Jesus did just that to heal a man born blind, it sent them into a tailspin. Jesus addressed this issue in another passage where He said, *"If one of you has a child or an ox that falls in a well on the Sabbath will you not immediately pull it out?"(Luke 14:5)* He tried to appeal to their common sense. He tried to help them understand that there are things that supersede rules. Things like love, compassion and humanity.

In the Old Testament after He set up the sacrificial system, man took it and turned an active, living, beautiful, hands-on expression of worship and turn it into dry, lifeless rules. God got so frustrated with them that in the first chapter of Isaiah He said He was sick of their offerings and He despised their incense. He went on to say in chapter 29, *"The*

Lord says: "These people come near to me with their mouth and honor me with their lips, but their hearts are far from me. Their worship of me is based on merely human rules they have been taught." God didn't set up rules just to have rules. He didn't set up rules just to be able to catch the wrong-doer and punish them. There was purpose and meaning behind them. There was prophecy and fulfillment in them. He didn't and doesn't just want blind, heartless obedience. He wants us all in, heart and soul.

When Jesus came down and became Man, he rolled up His sleeves and He got to work. I know He was thrilled to be hanging out with us, but He had something to do, a point to make. He redeemed mankind through His death on the cross. That was the thing He had to do. But what about the point He made? What about the meaning and heart that infused His life? In the 33 years before the cross He showed us what God was like. Jesus said, *"Anyone who has seen Me has seen the Father." (John 14:9)* Throughout His ministry Jesus showed us that God is loving and compassionate, not haughty, not untouchable, but approachable and kind. He showed us that God would do anything to be close to us, to be near us, even looking like an outcast, even breaking the rules. Nothing will hold Him back from getting to us. He would risk the wrath of the Pharisees, spit on the ground and get His hands dirty again to heal us. When you know that about God, when you embrace that about God, then the rules are easy, the rules make sense, the rules are infused and saturated with life and love.

When I ask people who I perceive as being "all in" or truly in love with Christ to tell me about their Faith, they don't often spout doctrine and theology or a list of rules. Often they put their hands over their hearts or grab their chests or they look up at the sky or close their eyes. Words don't come easily. They might mumble something about just knowing. Or they might say something very similar to the man born blind, *"Once I was blind, but now I see."*

When Jesus Cooked Breakfast

"Jesus said to them, 'Come and have breakfast."John 21:12

I recently had a very close friend pass away. I hung around the last week that she was alive and suffering to try to be of some help to her and her family. I made myself available to do whatever was needed. Often what was needed was to get food. During those emotional, trying times, food is usually the last thing on someone's mind until they realize that they're starving. So, I stood around and reminded people to eat and then offered to go get it.

Now that my friend is gone, there's a gaping hole left. There's left over time that I'm not sure what to do with yet. There's a surplus of love and care that I have no one to direct it toward. I find myself just sitting sometimes, just sitting and doing nothing. So, I think about what I did before she got sick and try to do those things. It's not the same.

The time between Jesus' death and His ascension is a very interesting time to me. I often wonder what that was like. I imagine it was a time of sadness – because everything had changed. I imagine that it was very confusing with Jesus showing up here and there and no one knowing what to do. I think the emotion that ruled the day was grief. The disciples were probably not eating and they were probably just sitting around. I think it was Peter who said, "Well, I'm going fishing!" When you don't know what to do, you do what you know, what's familiar. And Jesus, like the Good Friend He is, met them where they were and cooked breakfast for the guys. Jesus either brought some bread or created it, caught some fish, started a fire and the Lord of Lords and King of Kings cooked breakfast for His friends. He knew they were sad and confused. He knew they were probably not eating or sleeping. He understood their grief. He didn't reprimand them for going back to fishing. He didn't judge them for just sitting around on the boat. He just met them on the beach and made sure they had something to eat. If *"Jesus Christ is the same yesterday and today and forever" (Hebrews 13:8),* why do I think He's disappointed with me when I go through a time of grief and confusion? (Please excuse that little sermonette to myself).

After they ate breakfast and before Jesus headed off to heaven to take the place of honor at the right hand of God, He had to talk to Peter. Jesus couldn't leave without making sure that Peter was going to be ok. Peter had denied Him, yet He takes time to make sure Peter is ok. How He makes sure Peter is ok is the way He often helps me get over a personal failure. God puts me in a situation where I have to admit, confess or act on the Truth that I know. When I doubt His ability to heal, I will inevitably have to pray for someone's healing. When I struggle with whether He's real, I'll be in a situation where I have to convince someone else He is. So, in classic God fashion, Jesus asked Peter questions until Peter was able to proclaim what was in his heart, "Lord, you know I love you!" Jesus knew Peter loved Him, He just wanted to make sure that Peter knew it. Sometimes the greatest moments of healing, restoration and wholeness happen around a fire, a good meal or a walk on the beach. Jesus showed us that.

When God Lives With Us

"I heard a loud shout from the throne, saying, "Look, God's home is now among his people! He will live with them, and they will be his people. God himself will be with them." Revelation 21:3 (NLT)

I personally think that the verse above is the culmination of the Story, the reward, the victory, the purpose for all the blood, sweat and tears. God gets to hang out with us without hindrance, without sin, with complete and utter freedom! This is what God wanted all along.

I remember when I was dating my husband and we'd go out and have a great night and I would dread when we had to say goodnight. I hated it when he had to go to his house and I to mine. I remember lying in bed saying, "One day soon we won't have to say goodnight. We will never have to be separated again." I think that's how God has felt all along.

When that time comes, that time mentioned in Revelation 21 God will shout from His throne because He is so happy! He will finally get to hang out with us for all eternity! My mind goes crazy wondering what that will be like. In my opinion, I think it will be like it is now, only tremendously better! God is with me now, I sense His Presence. I know He is near. However, there is so much in our way. There's so much limiting our life together. He and I spend days together, we talk about things, we live life together, so that's the part I think will remain the same. God will always be the same. God is creative and active and so I believe eternity will be also. I think He wants to dream and plan and create with us like He has all along. Can you imagine, though, what we might create and do in a new heaven and a new earth? I can imagine a lot!

Once, when I was teaching fifth grade, I had a student who didn't want to think about heaven. I asked him why. He said that there was so much here on earth that he loved and didn't want to give up. I asked him for an example. He said, "Like my motorcycle. I don't want to give up my motorcycle." I responded with, "What if you don't have to give up your motorcycle in heaven, but rather you'd have a motorcycle that is better." He said, "Like how?" I said, "Like what if your motorcycle could fly? Or go faster than you can imagine without the danger?" His imagination took off and he then got excited about heaven. The Bible says, *"No eye has seen, no ear has heard, and no mind has imagined what God has prepared for those who love him." (1 Corinthians 2:9 NLT)* Why are we afraid to imagine? The verse says that no mind has ever imagined what God has prepared for us. It doesn't say we shouldn't imagine! So, when I see all these movies with computer graphics and all the crazy stuff people dream up, I always think, "But that is nothing like heaven."

I believe that God took great joy in creating the world in which we now live. I believe He hid treasures for us to find. Like a Father hiding gifts for his child, I believe God placed amazing creatures and plants in the oddest places and has stood back with joy watching us find them. God created such varied biomes and landscapes for our enjoyment. When great discoveries were made, I believe He cheered! When Jacques Cousteau developed SCUBA gear, I think God was on the edge of His throne waiting for us to find all the treasures He hid in the ocean. When space travel began, I think He couldn't wait for us to explore the heavens and was thrilled when our mouths dropped open in amazement. I don't think all that will stop in eternity. I think it will continue and be even better!

A lot of people believe that when we get to heaven we will just know all things. What about those of us who enjoy the journey of discovery and learning? I love libraries. I love history. Why can't heaven be a place where we meet people and learn from them? Why can't heaven be a place where we can finally see history clearly and accurately? I don't want to stop learning, so my personal dream of heaven is that learning will never stop.

I also think we will be in God's Presence constantly. Here, now, we only have that at times, in snippets. I think when we get to heaven it will be continuous. That's why we need new bodies. Our bodies and minds and hearts now can't contain the joy unspeakable and glory that will be our normal life up there. With that constant Presence, there will be peace and joy and the feeling that we're finally home. The place we were meant to be all along. All of us who have been without home and country or have lost loved ones will finally be reunited and arrive home. God will be there and we will be home. We will feel safe and loved. Oh to be there now!

All this desire I have to be there, to feel it, to know it, to have it, doesn't compare to God's desire to have us there. He's done all the work, all the sacrifice to get us there. He's the One who reached down, got His hands dirty to make it happen. All we have to do is believe. All we have to do is accept this Gift. How can we possibly refuse all of His love and care? I can't.

When God Met Me On The Beach

"For I am convinced that neither death nor life, neither angels nor demons, neither the present nor the future, nor any powers, neither height nor depth, nor anything else in all creation, will be able to separate us from the love of God that is in Christ Jesus our Lord."Romans 8:38-39

I want to tell you about the time when I couldn't refuse God's love. I got saved at 12 years old in a little country church in North Carolina. I wasn't taken to church very often so I'm not sure where the dress came from that I was wearing. I don't remember much about the service except the dress and the last few things the pastor said. He said, "If you have a loved one who has died and you would like to go to heaven to see them again, you need to come up here and accept Christ as your Savior." I remember that got my attention. My mother had died when I was 3 years old and I had no memory of her. I never knew her. I really wanted to meet her. I remember my heart beating fast and feeling a pull, a literal pull toward that altar and the pastor. I turned to my brother-in-law sitting beside me and said, "I think I need to go up there." He said, "Well, you better go then." I went up and prayed with the pastor and cried because my heart was bursting.

In the days, weeks and years that followed, I didn't feel much different, I'm sure I didn't act much different however, I had made a decision. I was a Christian. I went to church when I was allowed but that was about it. I had a little Bible that my brother gave me that I treasured. Mostly because he had given it to me but I didn't' really read it. I went through my teen years doing things I shouldn't be doing, going to church on weekends and asking for forgiveness for those things I knew I shouldn't have done. As time went on I got involved in a youth group where I was discipled in a deeper understanding and walk with Jesus. I began to take a more active and participatory role in my faith. As an older teen I had to make the hard choice between following Christ or following my friends. I chose Jesus and that's when I began in earnest to be a "good" Christian. I prayed, I read my Bible and I went to church. I made all those things a priority. However, no matter how hard I tried I always felt like I wasn't doing enough. I felt like I fell short of God's expectations somehow.

When I was 22 years old, after 10 years of trying to be a "good" Christian I was tired. I was tired of all the work and no reward. I was tired of feeling guilty all the time. I was tired of feeling "not good enough." I'm not sure what happened exactly but I got my feelings hurt by someone I really looked up to. They let me down. They hurt me. So, I used that moment to blame them and say, "If that's what a Christian is then I don't want to be one!" I decided to stop being a Christian.

I was driving down to Florida on a visit and I had a plan. I would stop by my favorite beach and say good-bye to God. I wanted an official ending to our relationship. I remember I parked my little, orange VW bug, took my shoes off and walked down to the beach. The beach was empty except for the large boulders that were scattered on the shore. I stood right at the edge of the water right where the surf touches your toes. I took a breath and before I could say anything I heard a voice. It was big and loud but I'm not sure if it came from outside my head or inside my head. I knew it was Jesus' voice even without Him identifying Himself. This is what He said:

"See that ocean?"

"Yes." I said.

"I made it for you because I knew you'd like it. On the day I made it I thought of you."

I was silent. Overwhelmed.

"Before you go, I just want you to know that I love you. I don't care if you ever read your Bible again or pray or go to church again. I just want you to know that I love you."

I fell to my knees. He loves me. That's all. He loves me. I cried. I don't know how long I was there on my knees in the sand overwhelmed with the love that rushed over me and in me. In one fell swoop Jesus took away all my reason for feeling guilty. He took away all the reasons for me to have to perform, to measure up to have to try to be a Christian. It wasn't about all the doing and trying. It was about love. It wasn't even about me loving Him. He loved me. I didn't have to do anything except be loved. God wasn't even bartering or manipulating or bribing me to stay. He said, "Before you go…" He wasn't trying to trap me or cage me. He was setting me free! I walked off that beach free from guilt, free from the burden of duty. I walked off that beach loved by an Almighty God who thought of me.

I have spent the last 32 years loving God back. Just like He thought of me, I think of Him in everything I do. I don't try to be a Christian anymore. I try to stay free. When I feel people or the church try to put rules and requirements on me, I quickly take them off. I will always remind myself of the simple truth that I learned that day on the beach: Jesus loves me, He thinks of me and He wants to hang out with me.

www.ingramcontent.com/pod-product-compliance
Lightning Source LLC
Chambersburg PA
CBHW061314040426
42444CB00010B/2644